BIG TRUTH little books®

What the Bible Says About Depression

Cliff McManis

GBF Press

Sunnyvale, California

What the Bible Says About Depression

What the Bible Says About Depression is volume 10 in the Big
Truth little books® series.

General Editor: Cliff McManis
Series Editor: Derek Brown
Associate Editors: J. R. Cuevas, Breanna Paniagua,
Jasmine Patton
Cover Design: Josh Weir

Dedicated to Americo and Isabelita,
dear saints who know the sufficiency
of joy in Christ

CONTENTS

SERIES PREFACE

Our mission with the *BIG TRUTH little books*® series is to provide edifying, accessible literature for Christian readers from all walks of life. We understand that it is often difficult to find time to read good books. But we also understand that reading is a valuable means of spiritual growth. The answer? Get some really big truth into some little books. These books may be small, but each is full of Scripture, theological reflection, and pastoral insight. Our hope is that Christians young and old will benefit from these books as they grow in their knowledge of Christ through his Word.

Cliff McManis, General Editor
Derek Brown, Series Editor

INTRODUCTION

Depression is real. Christians and unbelievers alike are plagued by it. This smothering malady is common among believers in the church. It overwhelms people and at times destroys lives. Depression is a complex topic.

While it seems most people would agree with the preceding statements, there are also important matters related to depression over which people bitterly disagree and share little to no common ground—even among Christians. Such bitterly contested topics can be delineated in the form of basic diagnostic questions, such as the following:

    (1) What is the definition of depression?
    (2) What causes depression?
    (3) How should depression be treated?
    (4) Who is qualified to treat depression?
    (5) Does the Bible talk about depression?
    (6) Do mature Christians get depressed?
    (7) Is depression a sin?
    (8) Is depression always bad?

Four Views

One need not look far before realizing that Christians don't all agree on how to answer the above eight diagnostic questions about depression. Christian leaders and teachers generally fall into four general camps when it comes to dealing with the ubiquitous problem of depression.

First, there are the *Integrationists*. This group consists of professing Christians who try to integrate evolutionary thought and secular psychology (or humanism) with the Bible to form a lens by which to diagnose and treat the problem of depression. These ecumenists attempt to mix the best of Freud with the best of Paul. They assume the Bible could use a little help from B. F. Skinner, Carl Rogers and Bob Newhart.

Second, there are the *Compartmentalists*. These professing Christians say that matters of depression and other emotional problems need to be delegated to the secular medical professionals, psychologists, and psychiatrists because the Bible does not address those matters. In other words, we need to compartmentalize various problems: some problems are spiritual while others are strictly psychological. Psychological problems, like depression, need to be farmed out to relevant specialists—the secular medical and health professionals.

Third, there are the *Idealists*. This group of professing Christians would argue that depression is exaggerated in most cases and is merely a manifestation of a hidden sin problem that needs to be exposed—the remedy for them is simple: "Repent and memorize this Bible verse!" This is the hard-nosed approach to dealing with problems. Or, it's the overly-simplistic approach to ministry—just telling people to suck it up and listen to more sermons. It's also the callous approach.

And then there is a fourth group of Christians—the camp I align with—that believes depression is real and that the Bible sufficiently addresses how it should be treated. I will call this group the *Traditionalists*, for lack of a better term. This is the traditional view for much of the Church age since the time the Bible was written—the view among God's people affirming that God's Word, written Scripture, sufficiently addresses all of life's problems, including depression, by principle, precept, promise, or picture. This little book will attempt to flesh out in greater detail this fourth option with the goal of providing practical help to believers who battle with depression.

Preliminary Observations

Before defining depression from a biblical perspective, it is first helpful to describe depression from the world's perspective—from a secular, humanistic, non-biblical viewpoint. There is much written on the subject—too much to read in fact. But we begin with some current agreed-upon statistics and trends.

1. *Depression is widespread in our world today.*
    Many researchers estimate that globally,
    350 million people per year say they
    suffer from depression from one degree
    to another. And they tell us there are at
    least 21 million people in the United
    States alone who struggle with
    depression each year. According to the
    World Health Organization, depression
    is the leading cause of disability
    worldwide and in the United States—an
    observation that is unanimous among
    many of the prominent journals and
    experts on this subject.

2. *Depression becomes dramatically manifest
    during the teenage years.* According to the
    leading medical journals, one out of five
    teens experience depression before
    adulthood. Suicide is a leading cause of
    death for teens currently. It is believed
    that a teen commits suicide every 100
    minutes in our country.

3. *Today, depression is primarily treated with
    antidepressants or pharmaceutical medication.*
    As a result, antidepressants are the
    second leading pharmaceutical drug in
    the world today. There are over two-
    dozen different antidepressant drugs,
    (one being Prozac) and many others
    with long names and many syllables that
    you may have never heard of.

4. *Each year, an estimated 40,000 people in the United States commit suicide.* In actuality, the numbers are probably far greater than this. The vast majority of these people suffered from some form of depression in one degree or another. The people who did commit suicide were known to suffer with depression and, on many occasions, had problems with drug or substance abuse.

5. *Generally, women admit to suffering from depression more than men.* This is something upon which almost all mainstream medical journals and experts agree. In the United States, women attempt suicide more than men, although more men are actually successful at carrying it out.

There are endless resources on this subject that one can research, but I eventually landed on three popular sources for the stats above: *The Stanford Medical Journal Online* and its authoritative study on depression; the official United States Government health site; and the *World Health Organization.* These three popular resources said virtually the exact same thing about depression: what it is, its manifest symptoms, a proposed diagnosis and how it should be treated.

Elusive Definitions

One of the biggest challenges in addressing this topic is developing a clear definition of what depression actually is. As a pastor, I have been counseling people with depression on a regular basis for over twenty years in different contexts and to varying degrees. And the greatest number of counseling scenarios I deal with are related to the topic of depression.

It is not uncommon for someone to come for counseling and then tell me their problem is "depression." I inevitably will ask, "What is depression?" I hardly ever get the same answer—the responses are all over the map. And when I ask the follow-up question, "What do you think causes depression?" the disparate answers abound even more; many times the counselee can't even answer that question. And sadly, most of these dear folks have been programmed by the world to believe that the only real solution is medication. But the main point here is that rarely does the person seeking help have an accurate, objective, biblical definition of depression. But one can't make a diagnosis, give a prognosis, or recommend a cure if one doesn't begin with a proper definition of the problem at hand. For this reason, it is vital to understand what depression is.

Formulating a clear and accurate definition of depression is no easy task. The "Christian" community does not have a homogenous definition of depression, as we saw previously. The secular world fares no better—they also have their competing factions, camps and schools of thought. Nevertheless, the most popular medical and health institutions in the secular world do have some complementary presuppositions that come to the surface upon close scrutiny. For illustration I have selected three such sources to highlight what the secular health experts have concluded about depression. These three sources include The World Health Organization (WHO), the American Psychiatric Association (APA), and the U. S. government's National Institute of Mental Health (NIMH). Consider their definitions of depression below.

1. World Health Organization (WHO): In its online source, WHO defines depression as follows:

> Depression is a common mental disorder, characterized by persistent sadness and a loss of interest in activities that you normally enjoy, accompanied by an inability to carry out daily activities, for at least two weeks. In addition, people with depression normally have several of the following: a loss of energy; a change in appetite; sleeping more or less; anxiety; reduced concentration; indecisiveness; restlessness; feelings of worthlessness, guilt, or hopelessness; and thoughts of self-harm or suicide. Depression is treatable, with talking

therapies or antidepressant med-ication or a combination of these.[1]

There are a few important details to note in this proposed definition. First, it is not really a definition; it is a description. The closest thing to a definition in the statement is when it says depression is "persistent sadness" that lasts "for at least two weeks." Second, most everything else in this paragraph is a delineation of symptoms, not a definition. Third, this definition states no *cause* for depression. Most technical defi-nitions of real, organic medical diseases include the cause of the ailment or condition.

2. American Psychiatric Association (APA): In answering the question, "What is Depression?" the American Psychiatric Association defines depression as follows:

> Depression (major depressive disorder) is a common and serious medical illness that negatively affects how you feel, the way you think and how you act. Fortunately, it is also treatable. Depression causes feelings of sadness and/or a loss of interest in activities once enjoyed. It can lead to a variety of emotional and physical problems and can

---

[1] www.who.int/mental_health/management/depression/en/.

8

decrease a person's ability to function at work and at home.[2]

This so-called definition is more of a description than a proper definition. And it makes two bold assertions that are misleading. First, it states that depression is a "medical illness," which I will dispute in this book. Depression is more than a medical illness; but I also believe it can contribute to causing other medical conditions and even illnesses.

The problem with the APA definition is in the statement, "Depression causes feelings of sadness." But just the opposite is true: feelings of sadness can cause depression. If one reads carefully, you will notice the APA definition never gives a proposed *cause* of depression, just as the WHO failed to do. But in the sentence we just examined the APA asserts that depression *causes* sadness.

3. National Institute of Mental Health (NIMH): The NIMH is a center sponsored by the US Health and Human Services. It is the primary governmental agency responsible for health-related research. This seventy-year-old, tax-payer-supported entity boasts of being the largest research organization in the world specializing in mental illness. Here's how they define depression:

---

[2] www.psychiatry.org/patients-families/depression/what-is-depression.

> Everyone feels sad or low sometimes, but these feelings usually pass with a little time. Depression—also called 'clinical depression' or a 'depressive disorder'—is a mood disorder that causes distressing symptoms that affect how you feel, think, and handle daily activities, such as sleeping, eating, or working. To be diagnosed with depression, symptoms must be present most of the day, nearly every day for at least 2 weeks.[3]

Like the two previous sources, the NIMH is scant on giving any substantive details in defining depression. Their proposed definition, like the others, is really a description more than a definition. The closest they get to defining depression is when they say it "is a mood disorder." The rest of the paragraph is given to describing the symptoms and effects of depression. It also contains a backwards and wrong assumption when it asserts that depression "causes distressing symptoms that affect how you feel, and think." Again, I would assert the converse: depression is caused by wrong thinking and emotions *that result in* distressing symptoms. In other words, I am arguing that these secular authorities on health and medicine are turned 180 degrees upside-down when trying to assess the complexities of depression.

---

[3] www.nimh.nih.gov/health/publications/depression/index.shtml

Another popular and authoritative source for information on health issues is WebMD. This respected source answers the question, "What is Depression?" as follows:

> when intense sadness—including feeling helpless, hopeless, and worthless— lasts for many days to weeks and keeps you from living your life, it may be something more than sadness. You could have clinical depression—a treatable medical condition.[4]

This brief paragraph proposes several notable elements that constitute a "definition" of depression from a secular, non-biblical perspective. According to WebMD, depression,

(1) is "intense sadness...something more than sadness"
(2) "lasts for many days to weeks"
(3) "keeps you from living your life"
(4) is synonymous with "clinical depression"
(5) is a "medical condition"
(6) is "treatable."

Like so many other alleged authoritative sources on depression, WebMD is thin on actually defining depression. In the above six elements, only point (1) hints at a real definition, and it's skimpy and general at

---

[4] www.webmd.com/depression.

best. Depression is "intense sadness." Points (2)-(6) are not definitions of depression, but rather elements of the pathology (effects), diagnosis (the symptoms) and prognosis (the proposed cure) of depression.

Of great significance here is that the WebMD "definition" does not include the cause of depression. The three other authoritative health sources mentioned earlier did not delineate a cause either. That is a problem. Research the basic definitions of most other known, real, organic medical illnesses and you will typically find the basic cause listed as part of the definition.

For example, in WebMD's definition of an ulcer, it includes the basic cause, noting that ulcers occur. "when your stomach acids etch away your digestive tract's protective layer of mucous."[5] This is true of the definitions of a hernia, a cavity, various cancers, the mumps, the measles and poison oak—real, *bona fide* medical conditions and illnesses. I propose that WebMD, the World Health Organization, the American Psychiatric Association and the U.S. National Institute of Mental Health don't include the cause of depression in their respective definitions of depression because they don't really know the cause of depression! Herein lies the problem and the debate about defining and treating depression. The Bible says

---

[5] www.webmd.com/digestive-disorders/peptic-ulcer-overview.

something radically different than the secular world about the cause, diagnosis, and cure for depression.

A Preliminary Biblical Definition of Depression

It is hard to find a clear, comprehensive, unifying definition among the proffered secular sources. One thing is clear from reading such literature: they conclude that one's spiritual condition has nothing to do with depression. Religion, faith and spirituality have been banished from their presuppositions about basic anthropology. According to the secular worldview, humans are not holistic, complex creations made as persons by the Creator, Judge and Savior of the universe. They are, rather, one-dimensional, naturalistic, evolved automatons. The consensus seems to be that depression is strictly limited to the medical sphere. The Bible says otherwise. God's Word has much to say about depression, *including* its cause. The rest of this book will be an exposition of what Scripture says about depression. Here I propose a preliminary definition of depression informed by biblical principles that we will look at in more detail. Depression includes the following:

(1) intense sadness, grief, or distress;
(2) to be deeply troubled in mind or thought life;
(3) to be emotionally distraught;
(4) to be overcome with hopelessness and loss of joy;

(5) all caused by various spiritual, cognitive and psychological factors.

A couple comments are in order about my five-fold preliminary definition of depression. First, I came up with the definition as a result of a thorough study of the Psalms, noting the dozens of Hebrew words that inform all manner of depression and distress that the various writers of the Psalms were experiencing at any given moment. The fact that the Bible uses dozens of different words and expressions to describe the reality of depression shows the complexity of the malady and should serve as a safeguard against positing one-dimensional and shallow diagnoses and remedies that are so common today. Below is a small sampling of the dozens of synonyms found throughout the Psalms that describe elements of human depression. The English word is underlined and the corresponding Hebrew term is to the right in bold:

"My soul is greatly dismayed" (6:3)....*bahal*

"I am weary with my sighing" (6:6)....*anachah*

"My eye has wasted away with grief" (6:7)....*ka'ac*

"the groaning of the needy" (12:5)....*anaqah*

"having sorrow in my heart all the day" (13:2)....*yāgon*

"In my <u>distress</u> I called upon the LORD"
(18:6)....*bassar*

"I am lonely and <u>afflicted</u>" (25:16)....*ani*

"The <u>troubles</u> of my heart are enlarged"
(25:17)....*tsarah*

"I am like a <u>broken</u> vessel" (31:12)....*abad*

"the <u>bereavement</u> of my soul" (35:12)....*shekol*

That is just ten examples of dozens that exist. In addition to the Psalms, pertinent passages from the rest of the Old Testament and the New Testament were also taken into consideration.

Second, it is significant that my definition of depression does not exclude the notion of "anxiety" as something altogether separate and distinct. In fact, I would argue that depression can include anxiety and often does. They overlap. This idea flies in the face of secular psychiatric orthodoxy of the past century. Secular psychiatrists and psychologists artificially dichotomize anxiety and depression, treating them as independent diseases like athlete's foot and lung cancer. But nothing could be further from the truth. According to the Bible, depression and anxiety have a common pathology in that both maladies frequently stem from unhealthy or defective thinking. Generally speaking, anxiety is fear (or wrong thinking) about the future and unknown events whereas depression is errant thinking about the past and regrets. Anxiety and depression go hand in hand and are two different sides of the same coin. God's solution for managing, battling and overcoming anxiety and depression entails a good dose of healthy biblical thinking (Phil 4:6-9), meditating on divine truth (John 8:32), and self-control of the mind (Gal 5:22-23; Rom 12:1-2). This is why Jesus said that basic to true spiritual maturity and balance is "loving God with all your mind" (Matt 22:37). So from a biblical perspective depression and anxiety are directly related to *thoughts in the mind* not *chemicals in the brain.* That's a big difference.

With the above working definition, we press on to chapter one as we contend with and expose common myths about depression that clutter the landscape of understanding on this matter.

1

COMMON MYTHS ABOUT DEPRESSION

We live in a day and age where we have too much information. Modern technology has enabled us to publish a deluge of books at an unprecedented rate on every conceivable topic. And the Internet provides more information than anyone can read in a lifetime. In addition, virtually anyone can write and say anything they want on the Internet, whether it is true or false. There is a proliferation of contradictory opinions online, much of which is passed off as factual or authoritative. This is especially true on the topic of depression.

Do a Google search of "depression" and one is overwhelmed with a mass of articles, links, blogs, stories, and opinions—too much information through which to wade and absorb. Very little of it is from a biblical perspective and much of it is misleading. Who can you trust when it comes to getting advice or help on the topic of depression? For the Christian the Bible is the starting point for reliable answers regarding life's problems, including matters related to depression. Before exploring Scripture, however, it will first prove helpful to expose some of the more popular and common myths about depression. This will help us navigate our way through the morass of endless opinions and contradictory pontifications on the issue of depression.

Myth 1: *There is a clear, universally agreed upon definition of what depression is among professional psychologists and psychiatrists.* A cursory overview of popular secular medical and psychological journals, some of which we just saw in the previous chapter, will quickly reveal that there is no universally accepted definition of depression, nor are the "experts" in sync about its cause or cure. This fact is important, because with any real sickness or disease—a genuine organic, biological, physiological illness such as strep throat, the mumps, chickenpox, or leukemia—there is a universally agreed upon definition. But that is not the case with depression—there is no universally agreed upon definition.

Myth 2: *Depression is to be diagnosed and treated from only a medical perspective.* This is stated in most of the professional secular journals available on the topic. These journals push the notion that the diagnosis of depression should be strictly from a medical point of view and, philosophically, considered from a naturalistic or Darwinian point of view. Depression is seen as nothing more than a physical disease. The myth here is that depression should be diagnosed and treated only from a medical perspective and not outside of that—like from a religious, spiritual or biblical perspective. Sadly, many in the church have bought into this unbiblical and humanistic perspective.

Myth 3: *Depression is an illness or disease.* This is a corollary to Myth 2. I would posit that depression is not an illness or disease, technically speaking. This is how the world, since the time of Sigmund Freud (1856-1939) in the early 1900s, has been successful in diagnosing many of the common plights of humanity and couching them in medical terminology. Historically, however, that wasn't always the case. For example, until modern times drunkenness was considered a sin and an immoral behavior. But since the time of Freud, it has been re-diagnosed, re-categorized, and labeled as a disease. That is what the world says. The Bible says that drunkenness is a sin (Eph 5:18; cf. Prov 20:1). It is common for the secular world to redefine behaviors the Bible labels as sin and slot them into new categories in the attempt to recast that which is inherently immoral as amoral and that which is evil as virtuous. In reality, depression has been around for a long time. It was not until the twentieth century that depression was, for the first time on a popular level, categorized in medical terms as an illness or disease. We will see from Scripture, however, that depression is not a physical disease. By saying that depression is not an illness or a disease, I'm not dismissing it, nor am I saying that it isn't real. Depression *is* real, and it affects a lot of people. And at times it is related to illness or a disease. For example, long-term, chronic depression can contribute to, or exacerbate, other illnesses and diseases. And other diseases can bring on bouts of depression in certain people. So depression and actual diseases are not always unrelated.

Myth 4: *Depression is caused by a chemical imbalance in the brain.* Whether it is from too much serotonin, not enough serotonin, dopamine, or whatever else, all we have to do is figure out a person's level of dopamine and serotonin and just add a little or take a little away and—poof! The experts believe we can heal depression by merely prescribing medication. I would argue that chemical imbalances can contribute to the problem and exacerbate the problem, but they are not the sole cause of the problem. Too many so-called "experts" today hold to this myopic view and are, as a result, making false promises to countless patients, telling them, "Just pop a pill and you can manage your depression." The marijuana craze has reached a fever pitch in our day as well, and sadly many are saying that depression can be treated effectively with medical weed, which is the opposite of the truth since it has been scientifically established that marijuana is a depressive, addictive drug containing the psychoactive, mind-altering chemical, THC, which is detrimental to the brain.

Myth 5: *Psychologists and psychiatrists are the only qualified experts in dealing with depression.* This myth is based on the faulty premise that humans are animals—the by-products of evolution—and, for this reason, exist merely as material beings, not spiritual beings. This myth also stems from the false presupposition of Myth 2 above that says depression is to be treated strictly from a medical perspective. The truth is, humans are made in God's image (Gen 1:26-27) and are physical as well as spiritual beings who need to be diagnosed accordingly. Secular psychologists and psychiatrists are inept when it comes to diagnosing the hurting spirit and soul of humanity.

Myth 6: *Pastors are not qualified to deal with serious depression.* I would say that Scripture expects pastors to be qualified to deal with the average case of depression. A pastor who is gifted, trained properly, and who has experience in ministry, can give quality help to the depressed. Sadly, there are those who call themselves pastors who have no business counseling the depressed, and they give good pastors a bad reputation. Much depression stems from how a person thinks, and the Bible has much to say about our thought life. Competent pastors, armed with the knowledge of God's Word, therefore, can be experts in dealing with certain kinds of depression.

Myth 7: *Depression is not a spiritual or theological issue.* It is very common to hear this argument—that depression is strictly a medical issue, it is strictly a physical issue, or it is strictly a physiological issue. Ironically, this myth is often propagated by psychologists and psychiatrists who would like to maintain a monopoly in the treatment of depression. After all, it is not uncommon for psychiatrists to charge their depressed "patients" anywhere from $200 to $800 dollars a session and to maintain the same depressed patients for decades...a very lucrative trade indeed.

Myth 8: *Depression is not in the Bible.* This is a myth we would expect to hear from unbelievers; amazingly, I have had many Christians tell me this over the years, including several people who have come to me for counseling seeking help...for their depression! The truth is depression is found *all throughout the Bible*. I would argue that the Bible is the authority on depression.

Myth 9: *Depression is a recent phenomenon.* This is a common notion among the secular experts like clinical psychologist Laura Smith, who alleges, "Depression rates continue to increase. And most experts believe the increase is real."[1] Actually, depression is not just now on the rise. The misnomer results from the ever-changing definitions assigned to depression by the ever-morphing humanistic disciplines of psychology and psychiatry. Freud did not diagnose depression for the first time in the 20th century. Depression has been around since the first human beings fell into sin.

Myth 10: *If you had everything you wanted, you would not get depressed.* This is a common American myth. "If I just had that...if my spouse just behaved this way...if my children just behaved this way...if I just had this amount of money...if I just could achieve this goal...if I just wasn't single...then I wouldn't be depressed." Those notions are false, but are nonetheless common.

Myth 11: *Christians agree on the definition, cause, and care for depression.* On the contrary, there is great disharmony, disunity, infighting, arguing, and debate that goes on in the Christian world about how to deal with depression, how to define it, how to approach it, and whether or not the Bible addresses it. We highlighted this in the Introduction.

Myth 12: *Biblical counselors do not believe in "mental illness."* There is a large population, in and outside the church, who routinely misrepresent Nouthetic counseling (also known as "biblical counseling"). The phrase

---

[1] *Depression for Dummies*, (Wiley Publishing: Indianapolis, Indiana 2003), 1.

"Nouthetic counseling" was coined by Dr. Jay Adams and is thoroughly explained in his landmark book called *Competent to Counsel (CTC)*, released in 1970.[2] "Nouthetic" is a compound word in the Greek New Testament (*nous* = 'mind' + *tithemi* = 'to place into') that means "to place into the mind" by speaking truth to someone by way of encouragement, exhortation or rebuke (cf. Rom 15:14). The word *nouthetic* has proven over the decades to confuse people, so the preferred phrase representing this approach is simply called "biblical counseling." Jay Adams has been mischaracterized on the issue of mental illness for almost fifty years, for he in fact does believe there is such a medical condition called "mental illness." Listen to him in his own words in 1970: "Organic malfunctions affecting the brain...validly may be termed mental illnesses."[3]

Myth 13: *Biblical counselors believe depression is simply sinful behavior.* Biblical counselors are frequently misrepresented, and this is the second most popular caricature I hear from fellow Christians, usually pastors. For years fellow pastors on occasion have told me that Jay Adams and his ilk believe depression is always the same—always a sin, and always requiring the same remedy. They aver that Jay Adams' remedy amounts to a callous, trite rebuke to the faithless, self-

---

[2] Jay Adams, *Competent to Counsel* (MI: Baker Books, 1970).
[3] Ibid., 28.

depressed counselee: "Suck it up; stop being depressed; memorize a Bible verse!" Nothing could be further from the truth. Depression is real, complex, has many causes, and is not always sinful. And a superficial, rote memorization of a Bible verse is not the solution. And Jay Adams never had such a shallow, heartless approach toward people.

Myth 14: *Biblical counselors do not believe in using medications.* Here is another red herring, smearing the reputation of true biblical counselors. There is a balance. Real diseases and organic problems may require appropriate medication. At the same time, the rule of the day is to over-medicate and give a pill for every problem with little discretion and routinely with no scientific diagnosis. Jay Adams said that we should treat true "sickness with medical means accompanied by prayer."[4] He also states, "not all medication is unnecessary"[5] and in fact, biblical counselors should not work with their patients in isolation for "Medical problems demand close cooperation with a physician."[6] So this oft-repeated mantra is a myth. I, along with many other biblical counselors, believe in using medications when appropriate for legitimate medical problems, as determined by a real medical doctor.

---

[4] Adams, *Competent to Counsel*, 108.
[5] Ibid., 142.
[6] Ibid., 268.

Myth 15: *Spirit-filled and mature Christians do not battle with or suffer from depression.* This false idea is peddled in many different ranks among the Christian community from health, wealth and prosperity teachers to Word of Faith teachers to mainstream evangelicals who say we need to be "happy, happy, happy all the time" and even write songs saying so. Christian Science holds the extreme position on this myth as that cult teaches that there are no real diseases—it's all in the mind.

Myth 16: *Depression is always a bad thing.* This is possibly the most controversial myth of all. I would posit that depression is not always a bad thing. According to experts, one of the main causes of depression is guilt. As such, the easiest way to get rid of depression is by smothering any guilt that one might have and retraining or even searing the conscience so that all remaining guilt is hidden and drowned out. In other words, guilt is "bad." I would say just the opposite: guilt is not always bad. As a matter of fact, guilt can be a gift from God.

Myth 17: *Telling a Christian who is depressed to pray and read the Bible is just a canned, ineffectual platitude.* I've heard this quite frequently. Some Christians get upset and frustrated with biblical advice regarding their depression. But the fundamentals of Christianity include talking to God in prayer and listening to God by reading His Word—that is where it starts. It is not a platitude, and it is insulting to God and His Word to suggest such a thing.

Myth 18: *Having depression is an excuse to justify sinful and wrong behavior.* If some senseless man goes and shoots seventeen school children to death, it is not uncommon for news stations and other secular media outlets to basically justify or water-down the cold-blooded killer's behavior because of an apparent struggle with severe chronic depression. And in such cases, they usually blame the society, the killer's parents, the weapon, or politicians they don't agree with for the murder—blame-shifting, the kind that began with Adam and Eve (Gen 3:12-13). In reality, the killer is fully responsible and accountable for his actions. Being depressed is never a reason to commit sin or to justify sinful behavior.

Whether you are thinking about this topic because of your own bouts with depression or because you are talking with or counseling a friend, it is vital to have a biblical perspective. Now that we have looked at the most common myths regarding depression, let's look at how the Christian should view this important subject in God's unchanging, sufficient, glorious Word!

2

DEPRESSION IN THE OLD TESTAMENT

Let's begin this chapter with a real-life conversation.

Me: So what can I help you with?

Counselee: I have anxiety, panic-attacks and depression.

Me: How long has this been going on?

Counselee: At least twelve years.

Me: Have you done anything before for these problems?

Counselee: Yes. I have a psychologist I see regularly and I have a psychiatrist I see once a month and I am taking several medications for my depression and anxiety.

Me: How long have you been taking the medications?

Counselee: For years.

Me: Is any of this treatment working?

Counselee: No, not really.

Me: Well then, let's look in the Bible to see how God's Word might help.

Counselee: What? The Bible doesn't say anything about this problem I have!

This was an actual conversation I had with an adult Christian years ago. This person was born into a Christian home and grew up as a believer. He went on to tell me dogmatically that the Bible does not address depression and anxiety. He was raised in the church and had heard preaching for three decades, and still concluded the Bible does not address this issue. Sadly he was not an exception to the rule; his response is actually representative of how many Christians think.

The subject of depression is all over the Bible. Believers must understand this before they can even begin to properly diagnose and treat the problem. From Genesis to Revelation, whether it is explicitly stated by name or manifest in someone's life or modeled in a solution or a cry of the psalmist's heart, depression is in Scripture. And amazingly, some of the most respected saints in the Bible struggled with depression just like real people do today. A brief survey of those who have gone before us will prove helpful and encouraging to see how they were overcome with depression and struggled through it with God's help.

The Scriptures Encourage

In Romans 15:4 the apostle Paul says, "For whatever was written in earlier times was written for our instruction, so that through perseverance and the encouragement of the Scriptures we might have hope." In this verse God makes an amazing promise about the Old Testament. Here Paul says the Scripture provides "encouragement" and "hope." What do depressed people need more than anything? Encouragement and hope! And the kind of encouragement and hope the Bible provides is supernatural, heavenly, lasting, and life-changing.

Nothing in the world can provide that kind of encouragement and hope. Pills and medication provide temporary numbing, escape, distraction...and some-times even dependency, debt and addiction. Psychol-ogists and psychiatrists provide futile human wisdom that can't penetrate the soul or override the real causes of depression. Rapid eye therapy (RET) provides a temporary false hope based on junk science and Darwinian presuppositions, namely that humans are no more than sophisticated animals who are the by-product of chance evolution. The Bible, on the other hand, is the living Word of God that never returns void (Isa 55:11) and penetrates to the deepest recesses of the human heart, soul and mind (Heb 4:12).

One of the benefits of reading the Old Testament is that the Christian can gain perspective and endurance. By God's intent and design, the believer can identify with the scenarios and the people of the Old Testament. The encouragement of the Scriptures feeds and heals the soul. If you are a believer who is depressed or discouraged, you need a big, ongoing dose of the encouragement of the Scriptures. What is the by-product when you immerse yourself in the Word of God, even when you don't feel like it? "That we might have hope," Paul writes. What is the diagnosis of a depressed person? *They don't have hope.* Hope comes from the encouragement of the Scriptures.

If you have been suffering from any degree of depression, you need to, as a child of God, rest in the truth highlighted in 2 Corinthians 7:6: "God comforts the depressed." The word for "depressed" here is the Greek word, *tapeinós*, and refers to "one who is brought down low with despair or grief." God promises to lift you up. If you are a believer, God the Father is your ultimate Counselor because He adopted you into His own family (Rom 8:15) and "He cares for you" (1 Pet 5:7). Jesus Christ is also your personal Counselor (Isa 9:6). The Holy Spirit is your Comforter, your Counselor, and the One who provides encouragement since He is your Advocate who lives in you and will never leave you (John 14:16-18).

If you are a believer and you own a Bible, get your nose in the Word of God, listen to it taught and preached, immerse yourself in the refreshing waters of God's truth. Let's look briefly at examples of some of the godliest people in the Bible who were challenged with depression, and even more importantly how God was their sufficiency in the midst of their discouragement.

Joseph's Life of Hardship and Betrayal

Joseph was the son of Jacob (Gen 37:3) who suffered greater hardship than most of us will ever know. He had ten older brothers who hated him, beat him up, tried to kill him, and eventually sold him into slavery (Gen 37:28; Acts 7:9) and spent two years in a dungeon for a crime he did not commit (Gen 41:1). Despite decades of suffering and injustice, Joseph was a man of faith (Heb 11:2) who trusted God.

If anyone had a cause to be depressed it was Joseph. In prison, Joseph was utterly deprived, isolated, forgotten, and forsaken. Yet because he knew God personally and trusted in Him no matter what, "God was with him and rescued him from all his afflictions" (Acts 7:9). Joseph could have grown depressed and bitter toward his brothers who tried to kill him, toward the Pharaoh who threw him in prison, and toward God for allowing all this to happen. But he didn't.

He did, however, experience tremendous emotional

turmoil as a result of the whole grueling experience when at last he confronted his brothers in Egypt thirteen years after his demise:

> Then Joseph could not control himself before all those who stood by him, and he cried, "Have everyone go out from me." So there was no man with him when Joseph made himself known to his brothers. And he wept so loudly that the Egyptians heard it, and the household of Pharaoh heard of it. Then Joseph said to his brothers, "I am Joseph! Is my father still alive?" But his brothers could not answer him, for they were dismayed at his presence. Then Joseph said to his brothers, "Please come closer to me." And they came closer. And he said, "I am your brother Joseph, whom you sold into Egypt. And now do not be grieved or angry with yourselves, because you sold me here; for God sent me before you to preserve life" (Gen 45:1-5).

A little later after their father Jacob died, Joseph again wept before his guilty brothers and said, "'you meant evil against me, but God meant it for good...So therefore do not be afraid'...So he comforted them and spoke kindly to them" (Gen 50:20-21).

A key lesson for believers from the life of Joseph is to realize that bad circumstances and evil treatment from others does not justify becoming chronically depressed or bitter. In the midst of trying circumstances, God can extend us "kindness" and "favor" (Gen 39:21) to see us through the trial, regardless of how bad things get. That is God's promise. Paul said to Christians, "May the God of hope fill you with all joy and peace as you trust in Him" (Rom 15:13). But you have to trust Him. If you blame others, get bitter, justify your bad attitude, blame the circumstances, complain and grumble, refuse to give Him thanks, or seek relief and comfort in other places rather than in Him, then He won't "fill you with joy and peace." It's that simple. Trusting God is a deliberate choice—and that choice can result in inexplicable joy.

David's Personal Anguish: A Look at the Psalms

Another example to learn from in the Old Testament is King David. Like Joseph, he also loved God and was a man of faith. But unlike Joseph, David was prone to more turbulent bouts of emotional inconsistency—including seasons of severe depression, anxiety and fear. David's writings, taken as whole, reveal a man after God's own heart, while at the same time picture a man who walked with feet of clay and who exuded the full gamut of human emotions. This biographical sketch of David's personality and temperament can be gleaned from the Old Testament Psalms, seventy-five percent of which are attributed to his name.

Psalm 32

Several years ago, I counseled a believer who was going through the most severe case of depression I had ever encountered. I listened as he told me his own diagnosis of why he was overcome with a kind of depression that had brought him near to the point of death! I asked several questions about what he was feeling, what thoughts were going through his mind, how he was conducting his daily life, and so on. After he described these things in detail, I immediately thought of Psalm 32 and began reading it to him. Psalm 32 depicts David in aguish from unparalleled depression to the point that it made him physically sick. After I finished reading the short Psalm to my friend, I asked, "Does this sound like you?" It did—he could totally identify with that Psalm.

Psalm 32 provides a close look at David after he had committed grievous sins. It is fresh after he committed adultery with Bathsheba, murdered her husband Uriah, and subsequently tried to cover it all up (2 Sam 11-12). He was a believer, the king of Israel, and leader of God's people. He was supposed to be the shepherd and prophet of God. He was a man of God, he loved God, and God loved him. But these were horrific sins in which he had been involved and had attempted to conceal. He was finally exposed by Nathan the prophet who put his finger in David's face and confronted him for his egregious sins.

I believe Psalm 32 was written during this one-year period when David was battling on the inside with severe, chronic, "clinical" depression. While reading this Psalm, pay attention to what he says because of his sin and the compromise in his life. Despite being forgiven for his sins, he is reflecting on what the turmoil in his life was like:

> How blessed is he whose transgression is forgiven, whose sin is covered! How blessed is the man to whom the LORD does not impute iniquity, and in whose spirit there is no deceit! (vv. 1-2).

David was forgiven. There were severe consequences for his sin, but he was forgiven, and he is now reflecting on what it was like and how depressed he was as a believer:

> When I kept silent about my sin, my body wasted away (v. 3a).

Sin can be a key cause of depression. When you are silent about your sin, running from God, hiding your sin from God, and ignoring your guilt, depression will often take root. Depression physically affects us, especially for prolonged periods of time. You lose your appetite. You can't sleep. And it gets worse as you spiral down. That is exactly what happened to David as described in Psalm 32. This had nothing to do with chemical imbalances—that was not the ultimate cause of his depression. He probably had chemical imbalances as his depression worsened, but it was not the root cause.

> When I kept silent about my sin, my body wasted away through my groaning all day long (v. 3b).

There was a continual, unbroken, ongoing groaning in his soul that was akin to what today is called "chronic depression." For David, there was no human solution. Nobody could comfort him with mere human wisdom.

> For day and night Your hand was heavy upon me (v. 4a).

In other words, day and night he was being pressed down by God's judgment. God was chastening him for unconfessed sin. He describes it as God "pressing down" on him. That is depression. Not every cause of depression is a bad thing; sometimes God causes depression from His holy, purifying discipline. That is what this verse says. God disciplines those whom He loves (Heb 12:6). Day and night God's heavy hand was pressing down upon him, literally crushing him down, trying to get David to fess up and repent.

My vitality was drained away (4b).

This is common of somebody who has chronic, clinical depression—they lose strength and desire in every area of life, and that is what happened to David. He is the poster child of psychotic neurosis, major depression, bipolar disorder, or whatever you want to call it.

> I acknowledged my sin to You, and my iniquity I did not hide; I said, "I will confess my transgressions to the LORD"; and You forgave the guilt of my sin. Therefore, let everyone who is godly pray to You in a time when You may be found. Surely in a flood of great waters they will not reach him (vv. 5-6).

In these two verses David reveals the solution to the depression he endured for almost a year—a full, honest confession of his sin that he was hiding. And his advice to other believers is to pray to God and confess your sin before it is too late.

Psalm 38

Psalm 38 is another wonderful Psalm of David that deals directly with this topic. In this Psalm David pours out his heart in a uniquely transparent prayer that God has seen fit to preserve for us in Scripture so that we might learn from it and be encouraged by it.

Note some of the highlights.

> Oh LORD, rebuke me not in Your wrath,
> and chasten me not in Your burning anger.
> For Your arrows have sunk deep into me,
> and Your hand has pressed down on me
> (vv. 1-2).

The phrase "pressed down on me" is key, because that is the very etymology of the word "depression" in our English language—to press down; to smother; to suffocate. That is what God was doing to David. He was incredibly depressed; he was chronically depressed. He was aware of his depression at the time that he wrote this Psalm, and he even knew the cause of his depression: God! That's not something you're likely to hear anywhere else.

> There is no soundness in my flesh because
> of Your indignation; there is no health in
> my bones because of my sin (v. 3).

David was in a prolonged period of feeling depressed that began to affect him physically. That is what happens with depression—a depressed person can lose sleep, lose their appetite, and then spiral down physically. That happened to David.

> For my iniquities are gone over my head; as
> a heavy burden they weigh too much for me
> (v. 4).

David here explains the cause—guilt was causing his depression, and sin was causing the guilt. Guilt was acting like a barometer of the soul, and as a result David was discouraged. He is distressed. It seems that he is without hope for a moment.

> My wounds grow foul and fester because of my folly. I am bent over and greatly bowed down; I go mourning all day long (v. 5).

In other words, his depression is continual; it is chronic. In today's world, this "patient" would be checked into the ER and then rushed away to the psych ward where they would label him a bi-polar schizophrenic who needs to be on lithium and Seroquel daily for the rest of his life, at ever-increasing levels, as prescribed by his life-long psychiatrist, while meeting monthly with his psychologist who manages the cognitive behavioral therapy (CBT) indefinitely. But here David shows clearly that not all depression is a mere disruption of chemicals and synapses in the brain—some depression results from unconfessed sin and the loving chastening of the holy Creator. And sadly, you won't hear this diagnosis at the typical local Christian Counseling Center, either.

David goes on:

> For my loins are filled with burning, And there is no soundness in my flesh. I am benumbed and badly crushed (vv. 7-8a).

David's feelings are numb. He has no joy, no peace, no ambition, no motive, and no sense or purpose for living, at least in this moment. That is the very definition of depression.

> I groan because of the agitation of my heart (v. 8b).

The phrase "agitation of my heart" is translated different ways in various English versions. It is the very definition of a panic-attack. David's heart is pulsating at an unnatural and unhealthy level due to his distress, grief, hopelessness, fear, and anxiety. And as a result, he groans—his depression is literally manifest tangibly in his physical body. His distress then reaches a crescendo:

> For I am ready to fall, and my sorrow is continually before me. For I confess my iniquity; I am full of anxiety because of my sin (vv. 17-18).

This is an important passage because it serves as an excellent example of how the Bible addresses and illustrates depression. This is vitally important for pastors, as they have to address this issue with their people. *Depression is in the Bible.* But I would say this isn't just a case of depression; this is the worst order of depression. And this is not the depression of an unbeliever, but of a believer. Christians can suffer with depression just as David did. Fortunately, the psalm doesn't end there. David knows only God can pull him out of the mire of distress and gloom.

> For I hope in You, O LORD; You will answer, O LORD my God...Do not forsake me, O LORD; O my God, do not be far from me! (vv. 15, 21).

The life of David teaches us some important truths about depression that we don't hear anywhere else today. David's psalms remind us that some depression can be the result of unconfessed sin. And some depression is not merely medical—it is spiritual and moral. Some depression is alleviated when a person confesses sin to God. Guilt is not to be ignored nor despised, but is the by-product of the conscience. And the conscience is a gift from God given to every human at creation as a result of being made in His image (Gen 1:26-27; Rom 1-2).

Job's Unprecedented Trials

One of the oldest and longest books in the Bible is Job. It offers much to inform our thinking on the topic of depression because the main character in the book was subjected to greater hardship than the average person will ever experience.

Job was a godly man (Job 1:1), yet he was suddenly overcome with a flurry of devastating events including robbery and the loss of nearly all his personal property (1:13-17). Furthermore, all ten of his children were killed (1:2, 18-19), he contracted boils from head to toe (2:7), his wife spurned him (2:9), his closest friends gave him bad advice (42:7) and behind the scenes he was being oppressed by Satan himself (1:9; 2:4).

Job was suffering such excruciating physical pain (2:13) as well as emotional pain from all his trials that he cursed the day of his birth (3:11). He was so depressed that he was "bitter of soul" (3:20) and longed for death (3:21). In other words, Job was suicidal.

There is no greater sign of depression than being suicidal. Job's life was typified by "groaning... cries...fear...dread...not at rest...turmoil" (3:24-26). He further claimed to have "vexation...terrors...despairing" (6:2, 4, 14). He said for months, "My flesh is clothed with worms and a crust of dirt; my skin hardens and runs" (7:3, 5). The longer it went on the more Job loathed his life, gave full vent to his complaining and had deep bitterness in his soul (10:1). But through it all he never abandoned his belief in God, even though he argued with Him about his circumstances. All through the turmoil he realized that the way he felt was not due solely to a medical condition; he knew he was in a spiritual battle and his thought life was at the center of that conflict.

In the end Job allowed his thinking to be corrected and his perspective to be brought to "true North" (42:1-2). He humbled himself before God (42:6) and realized that despite his bad circumstances he still needed to trust in God's sovereignty and goodness. As a result the LORD blessed Job (42:12) and saw him through his emotional duress and season of depression.

Other Old Testament Saints

The Old Testament provides many other examples of believers who battled with anxiety, panic attacks, and depression. We could have given many more examples from the life of King David like when he feigned insanity out of "great fear" he had for Achish, king of Gath. As a result, David had an explosive schizophrenic, bi-polar episode as "he disguised his sanity before them, and acted insanely in their hands, and scribbled on the doors of the gate, and let saliva run down his beard" (1 Sam 21:13).

And there was the great prophet Elijah who at the peak of his ministry was overwhelmed by anxiety and became depressed to the point of no longer wanting to live. The Bible says, "he requested for himself that he might die, and said, 'It is enough; now, O LORD, take my life'" (1 Kings 19:4)!

Then there was Jeremiah the "weeping prophet," or the "depressed prophet," who for over fifty years preached under duress and rejection from the people. He described himself as one whose eyes were "a fountain of tears, that I might weep day and night" (Jer 9:1; cf. 13:17; 14:17). He wrote Lamentations, an inspired journal of one tormented with deep grief and anguish.

And don't forget Jonah the prophet who was prone to episodes of temperamental chaos and debilitating depression, at one point begging "with all his soul to die, saying, 'Death is better to me than life'" (Jon 4:8).

All the above references to the saints in the Old Testament clearly illustrate that depression is frequently found in the Bible among God's people. And as a result, what Paul said in Romans 15:4 is true: believers can go to Bible when they are discouraged so that through "the encouragement of the Scriptures we might have hope."

3

DEPRESSION IN THE NEW TESTAMENT

Peter the Apostle Experienced Depression

Just like the Old Testament, the New Testament is no stranger to depression. A fisherman, Simon Peter, was the head of Jesus' twelve apostles. He was vocal, impetuous, emotional, courageous, bold, and the best thing of all, saved by grace (1 Pet 1:3). He was a dynamic, colorful personality. And he had his ups and downs.

Peter too often gets a bad rap from Bible teachers and preachers. He had his faults, but he knew and loved God (John 21:17). From the very beginning when he was called by Jesus to follow Him, Peter answered with great humility and faith. And he knew he was not worthy because he was acutely aware of his sin. When seeing the glory of Christ revealed for the first time Peter was overwhelmed with a holy fear.

Luke explains it: "But when Simon Peter saw that, he fell down at Jesus' feet, saying, 'Go away from me Lord, for I am a sinful man!'" (Luke 5:8).

Peter was privileged to walk and talk and be discipled by Jesus for over three years. Nevertheless, because Peter walked with feet of clay like we all do, he was prone to bouts of fear (Luke 5:10), insecurity (John 16:16-18), lapses of faith (Matt 14:31), panic-attacks (Matt 16:22-23), delusion (Matt 26:33), and even depression.

Peter's greatest experience with depression was no doubt at the time of Christ's arrest and death. Peter's Lord, Rabbi, and friend had been suddenly snatched away without cause. Peter was confused and afraid during that period. When Jesus was arrested and undergoing trial, Peter was tormented with fear and denied Christ three times. He "began to curse and swear" when others questioned if he knew Jesus (Matt 26:74). After denying Jesus three times "he went out and wept bitterly" (Matt 26:75). Paralyzed with sorrow, Peter would hide in isolation for the next few days. On Resurrection Sunday morning Peter initially refused to believe Martha's testimony declaring Jesus was risen (Matt 28:11). But Peter came around. God helped him persevere (see Luke 22:31-32).

At Pentecost Peter helped found the Church and became one of its primary leaders. For the next thirty years he would remain steadfast, despite ongoing persecution from hostile unbelievers and conflicts within the church. Peter would eventually be murdered by Nero in the mid 60's AD. But through it all, he knew faith in Christ was the only thing that provided stability in this fallen world and only Jesus was a reliable anchor for the soul. Before he died he wrote to distressed fellow believers to encourage them, reminding them that life was hard:

> Beloved, do not be surprised at the fiery ordeal among you, which comes upon you for your testing, as though some strange thing were happening to you; but to the degree that you share the sufferings of Christ, keep on rejoicing, so that also at the revelation of His glory you may rejoice with exultation (1 Pet 4:12-13).

Peter could legitimately counsel and encourage anxious, frightened, depressed Christians because he went through similar experiences. And he knew first-hand that God was committed to helping believers persevere through the trials and hardships of life. And amazingly, God has promised in His Word to give real joy in the very midst of the worst of trials and hardships to those who trust Him.

Paul Faced Times of Depression

Who was the greatest Apostle? If you don't say Peter then you'd probably say Paul, and for good reason. Paul was the apostle to the Gentiles (Rom 11:13). A former Christian killer (1 Tim 1:13), he planted many churches during a ministry that lasted over four decades. He penned thirteen of the twenty-seven New Testament books. In many ways, Paul was incomparable and inimitable as a Christian, missionary, theologian, prophet, shepherd, and man of God. Yet he also walked with feet of clay, had his weak moments (Acts 23:3-5), battled with indwelling sin (Rom 7:14-25) was routinely discouraged and, at times, depressed.

Over a thirty-year period Paul travelled thousands of miles making a priority of evangelizing in towns and cities that never heard the gospel of Christ. He would preach to Jews in synagogues (Acts 17:2) and to Gentiles wherever he could find them (Acts 13:46). The response to his message and ministry became predictable: a few were intrigued, a few believed, and many were overtly hostile. He was routinely chased out of town (Acts 17:10). He was mocked, threatened, slandered, arrested, whipped, imprisoned, and even stoned to the point of death. Over the years, many professing Christians who once called him a friend abandoned and betrayed him (2 Tim 4:14, 16). Paul's whole Christian life and ministry was one mostly of hardship (1 Tim 1:12; 2:9).

Paul had great successes and victories as well, but he was also realistic about life—living in this sinful and fallen world is arduous. Twenty years after being saved and ministering as a church-planting apostle, Paul wrote 2 Corinthians around AD 56. As his most personal and autobiographical letter, this book reveals much about the details of Paul's suffering and also his mental state during times of duress. In 2 Corinthians we learn first-hand that depression was often Paul's companion. He opens the letter writing to fellow Christians by saying he recently was at the point of discouragement so severe that he even despaired of life itself:

> For we do not want you to be unaware, brethren, of our affliction which came to us in Asia, that we were burdened excessively, beyond our strength, so that we despaired even of life (2 Cor 1:8).

Here Paul is being honest about his emotional weakness, and he admits he was distressed to the point of wanting to die. This is the severest form of depression in this life. Earlier, we saw how other godly believers got so low in life they wanted to die: Job, Jeremiah, Elijah, Jonah. And now even the great apostle Paul! But as a believer who knew the God of the universe personally through faith in Christ, Paul depended on God to deliver him through his rock-bottom time of depression. And God was true to His promises:

> indeed, we had the sentence of death within ourselves so that we would not trust in

ourselves, but in God who raises the dead; who delivered us from so great a peril of death, and will deliver us, He on whom we have set our hope. And He will yet deliver us, you also joining in helping us through your prayers, so that thanks may be given by many persons on our behalf for the favor bestowed on us through the prayers of many (2 Cor 1:9-11).

For decades Paul's life was full of hardships, just like Joseph in the Old Testament. And just like Joseph he faced life's trials with the one thing—the only thing—that could rescue him from depression at the deepest level, and that was his faith, his view of ultimate reality, and his love for God's truth:

But we have this treasure in earthen vessels, so that the surpassing greatness of the power will be of God and not from ourselves; we are afflicted in every way, but not crushed; perplexed, but not despairing; persecuted, but not forsaken; struck down, but not destroyed (2 Cor 4:7-9).

Few Christians will ever endure the kind of hardship, trials and suffering that Paul was subjected to, but every believer can adopt Paul's perspective on living in a fallen world to find relief in the worst of circumstances. He writes,

Therefore we do not lose heart, but though our outer man is decaying, yet our inner man is being renewed day by day. For momentary, light affliction is producing for us an eternal weight of glory far beyond all comparison, while we look not at the things which are seen, but at the things which are not seen; for the things which are seen are temporal, but the things which are not seen are eternal (2 Cor 4:16-18).

Paul lived in tension. He had an internal, inescapable joy that came from knowing Christ. At the same time he often experienced dejection due to his own failures, the reality of demonic forces, the hostile sin of others, and living life on a cursed earth. His secret was that he welcomed both realities. He was not an idealist or a shallow optimist. He lived in light of how God has defined reality in His Word. Because of this, he could live in light of the greatest antinomy or paradox, as he declared he was "sorrowful yet always rejoicing" (2 Cor 6:10). We can learn much from Paul's walk of wisdom.

Jesus, Man of Sorrows, Acquainted with Grief

Years ago, I preached a series of sermons on "What the Bible Says About Depression." In one of the sermons I said, "Jesus got depressed." I even shared a Bible verse to back it up. The next day, I got reamed with a sharp email from someone in the congregation because of that statement. This person was furious, and the essence of his complaint went like this: "Pastor, did I hear you say yesterday that 'Jesus got depressed?' I can't believe it if you said that. Jesus never sinned and He was perfect. Depression and anxiety are sins, therefore there is no way Jesus ever got depressed!"

We had a back and forth email exchange and even some personal conversations on the matter, but in the end he was not convinced. He adamantly maintained, "Jesus NEVER got depressed!" How depressing....

It is true that Jesus was perfect and sinless (1 Pet 2:22) during His thirty-three years on earth. And it is true that worry and depression can sometimes be related to sinful thinking or sinful behavior. But I also maintain that according to the Bible there are times when Jesus experienced depression.

Jesus was full deity (John 1:1) and in the incarnation He took on full humanity (John 1:14). As a real man, He had a genuine human nature, and He experienced the full spectrum of human infirmities: His body got tired (John 4:6), hungry (Matt 4:2), and thirsty (John 19:28). He grew up as a child and went through the normal human maturation process (Luke 2:52). He felt joy, anger, sadness, and desperation—all human emotions. He was even tempted in all ways that we are, yet without sin (Heb 4:15).

The critical congregant I mentioned above was wrong on two counts when he insisted that Jesus never experienced depression. One, he assumed that all depression is a direct result of sin, but it is not. And two, his view of Jesus' deity did not allow for a biblical view of Jesus' humanity. Jesus was fully God and fully human. When you overemphasize one at the expense of the other you end up with a heretical view, or, at least, an unbalanced view of Jesus.

Actually, there is a third reason he was wrong—the Bible actually says Jesus got depressed. After the Last Supper, Jesus took His disciples to the Garden of Gethsemane to pray. Jesus would be betrayed by Judas, the other eleven disciples would scatter and abandon Him, and He would soon be subjected to beatings and crucifixion. And the worst torment yet to come would be absorbing the full fury of the Father's wrath as a substitute for sinners while on the cross (Isa 53:4-6). With all that to shoulder, Jesus reached the greatest level of human distress possible, or ever known.

Matthew says at this time in Gethsemane He took Peter, James and John with Him "and began to be grieved and distressed" (Matt 26:37). The Greek word for "grieved" is from the verb *lupeo* and means "sorrow." The parallel passage in Mark says Jesus "began to be very distressed and troubled" (14:33). The word for "distressed" here is the Greek verb *ekthambeo* and means "bewilderment" or "to be terrified." Both Matthew and Mark also use the word *ademoneō* which means "be in anxiety, be distressed, deeply troubled."

In the next verse in Matthew, Jesus elaborates on the nature of His emotional distress: "Then He said to them, 'My soul is deeply grieved, to the point of death'" (Matt 26:38). No human has ever experienced this level of emotional turmoil. This was depression of the first order. Jesus was not in a state of sin during this depression. He was simply living the reality of the human experience in the frailty of human emotion.

This episode in the garden is not the only time Jesus experienced severe distress and depression. Isaiah 53 predicted the Messiah would be familiar with sadness and emotional turmoil, for the Messiah was to be "despised and forsaken of men, a man of sorrows and acquainted with grief" (53:3). The feeling of human depression came with the role of being the "Suffering Servant."

When Jesus experienced distress, dejection or depression He dealt with it properly. He sought His Father in prayer for perseverance, comfort, and relief (Matt 26:36). He did not blame others. He did not blame His circumstances. He did not become idle and unproductive. He did not depend on others to coddle Him. He did not seek quick superficial relief. He did not resort to alcohol or numbing His feelings in harmful ways. He did not take his own life like Judas did (Matt 27:3-5). He welcomed the trials and the disappointing circumstances and lived through the pain.

When a person is distressed or faced with depression, there is a temptation to respond the wrong way—to sin in the depression or in light of the depression. Jesus felt those temptations, but refused all of them. As our great High Priest, Jesus can sympathize with our weaknesses...even depression; for He "has been tempted in all things as we are, yet without sin. Therefore let us draw near with confidence to the throne of grace, so that we may receive mercy and find grace to help in the time of need" (Heb 4:15-16).

Contrary to what many believe, depression is in the New Testament. And it is not relegated to some obscure passage, but seen vividly in the life of the greatest of the apostles, Peter and Paul, and even exhibited in the life of Jesus the sinless Savior. Because of this, the Bible can help us talk honestly about the nature and occasions of depression, and, more importantly, how we might find relief as modeled by the apostolic saints and Christ Jesus Himself.

4

BIBLICAL REASONS FOR DEPRESSION

From a survey of the whole Bible it is possible to suggest several causes of depression. Remember from the first chapter of this book, when we looked at authoritative secular sources about the definition of depression, these sources did not include a cause for depression. The closest they came was to call it a medical condition or a "mental illness." There are actually many contributing factors to depression. Following are several illustrated in Scripture.

Unconfessed Sin

Sin is not the only cause for depression, but it can be a major factor in many cases. This reality is virtually ignored in secular psychology and psychiatry. Earlier in this book we observed the detrimental effects of unconfessed sin in Psalms 32 and 38. When David tried to hide his sin from man and God he was smothered with anxiety, distress, and a lack of joy. In Psalm 51, he relays how his transgressions, sins, and evil behavior sapped him of his joy. Only after he fully repented and told the truth about his adultery did God restore his "joy and gladness" (v. 8).

Non-Christians harbor the worst unconfessed sin of all—suppressing the truth of God (Rom 1:18) and rejecting Jesus as Lord (John 3:18-20). Unbelievers will never have true joy or relief from ultimate depression in this life until they repent of their sins and embrace Christ as Savior and Lord. Unbelievers can't know true joy apart from Christ, and, as a result, they live in darkness, meaninglessness, and under the constant wrath of God (Rom 1:18). John 3:36 is clear: "He who believes in the Son has eternal life; but he who does not obey the Son will not see life, but the wrath of God abides on him." The word for "abides" here is *menō*, and in the present tense means the word gives the sense of "continues unabated." In other words, unbelievers can't shake the wrath of God pressing down on them because of their unbelief. Only salvation in Christ will provide the supernatural relief they need.

Ignorance About Sin

Many Christians are not fully aware of their sin and its attendant consequences. This can be a great cause of sorrow and depression in the life of a believer, particularly among newer believers, and especially those who get saved later in life. Christians are often not aware that sin permanently lives in the believer (Rom 7:21) and produces a daily spiritual civil war in the soul. The presence of this "war" can confuse many children of God. As believers they want to please God and forsake sin, yet sinful habits seem to continually hound them. As a result, believers may experience tremendous guilt and discouragement due to their residual sin. Read Romans 7:14-25 and see how frustrated the apostle Paul is with his own indwelling sin that he can't shake while in this life. He gets disgusted with himself, crying out, "Who will set me free from the body of this death?" (Rom 7:24). Only resurrection in the future will remove the presence of sin.

Ignoring Guilt

Many people have depression because they don't deal with guilt properly. All three secular health organizations referred to in the introduction of this book say that guilt is bad and needs to be eradicated. In other words, they argue that guilt is an illegitimate feeling that needs to be dismissed, justified, smothered, or ignored. They surmise that guilt is an unhealthy by-product of oppressive social norms foisted upon individuals, shackling natural inhibitions and liberties that should be expressed with full vent and no shame. In effect, they argue for no moral restraints. The Bible, on the other hand, says we should exercise self-control (2 Pet 1:6), deny ourselves (Luke 9:23), make war against our bodily passions (Col 3:5), put to death our lusts (Ro 6:13) and welcome guilt as a gift from God as a barometer of our conscience (2 Tim 1:3) and an internal signal that our thinking or behavior is out of sync with God's Law or Spirit (Rom 7:22). This notion of subverting guilt at all costs comes from the atheist Sigmund Freud and should be rejected outright.

Wrong Thinking

Many people have unmet expectations. They are depressed about their marriage or depressed about their family. They may be depressed about their kids or depressed about their job. They might be depressed about their lot in life. This comes down to unmet expectations. People need to be realistic about life and think about reality from a biblical point of view. This world has been subjected to futility by God from the beginning after Adam and Eve sinned (Rom 8:18-26). As a result, we all live in a fallen world, among fallen people. This life is full of "groanings" (Rom 8:26) and troubles (Job 5:7). Heartache, trials and pain are normative for all humans (Jam 1:5)—no one is exempt or is subjected to anything uncommon that the rest of us don't experience (1 Cor 10:13).

We are all emotional beings and naturally go through the full gamut of emotional experiences. Feeling sad, anxious or depressed once in a while should not be eschewed or avoided at all costs, or always drowned out with foreign meds or toxins to hide in the false, temporary, numbing world of escape. It is actually healthy to go through the full range of emotional experience, including deep sadness. In the Old Testament, God actually had designated extended periods of mourning for His people when it was appropriate. Thirty days of mourning were recognized by the Israelites when Moses died (Deut 34:8). Joseph and the Egyptians mourned for seventy-seven days when Jacob died as "they lamented there with a very great and sorrowful lamentation" (Gen 50:3-10). Depression and sadness are actually appropriate feelings to experience in light of the hardships of this life as we wait for the glories of heaven, when finally all sorrows and mourning and depression will be wiped away (Rev 21:4; 2 Cor 4:17).

Human Weakness

You can be depressed simply as a result of human weakness and frailty. The constitution of our present fallen bodies and minds make us all vulnerable to times of sadness, anxiety and depression. In 1 Corinthians 15, Paul says our present bodies are weak and frail (vv. 42-48). And some people are weaker in constitution and in personality than others. Some people are simply more prone to depression than others. In 1 Thessalonians 5, Paul reminds believers to "encourage the fainthearted, help the weak" (v. 14). Here he is referring to some people who struggle in this area of physical and emotional weakness. Peter reminds husbands that their wives are the "weaker" vessels (1 Pet 3:7), meaning women are emotionally more vulnerable and need to be protected accordingly. This is consistent with yearly statistics that continue to say that women attempt suicide more frequently than men and struggle with depression more than men, even though more men are successful at actually killing themselves. So, knowing your own temperament and your weaknesses can be a big help in combatting depression in your own life.

Demonic Oppression

Satan is a real personal being—and utterly wicked just as the Bible depicts (1 Pet 5:8). He is called "the accuser of the brethren" (Rev 12:10) because he ceaselessly harasses the children of God. Satan's assaults were a great cause of sorrow and depression in the life of Job (Job 1-2). Demonic spirits terrorized King Saul, greatly affecting his emotional state (1 Sam 16:14). In the New Testament, Satan and his demons indwelt and possessed people, causing serious oppression in their lives (Matt 8:22). In our current day, secular medical professionals completely ignore the reality of demons and the effect they can have on people, including depression; and some in the Christian charismatic world go to the opposite extreme, blaming demons for every problem in life, including post-nasal drip. The balance is somewhere in between—demonic oppression is real, causes depression, and is a real threat in the life of unbelievers (John 8:44; Eph 2:1-2).

Fear and a Lack of Faith

Hopelessness is at the root of depression; but so is fear. Fear is an illegitimate frame of mind about the future and demonstrates a lack of faith in God's desire or ability to act according to His promises. To fear is to not trust God.

Fear also sends the emotions into a tailspin. From Genesis (15:1) to Revelation (2:10), God commands His children not to fear, but rather to trust and rest in Him. God promises to provide supernatural internal peace to those who trust in Him rather than live in fear: "I sought the LORD, and He answered me, and delivered me from all my fears" (Psalm 34:4). Three times in Matthew 6 Jesus commanded His disciples, "Do not worry!" These are imperatives, not suggestions. We worry when we lack faith, so we need supernatural faith to overcome worry. Supernatural faith comes from only one place—the Scriptures: "Faith comes by hearing a word about Christ" (Rom 10:17). Do you want to guard against depression that many times is a result of fear and a lack of faith? Then consume God's Word as found in Scripture so He can strengthen you from the inside out with the power of His Spirit. There is no better solution.

So, who will you believe? The secular, humanistic, Freudian professionals who say you are nothing more than an animal, a result of millions of years of chance evolution made of mere matter and having no eternal purpose for your existence, who can numb emotional dysfunction by merely taking a mind-altering pill? Or will you believe in God who said in His Word that you were made in His image, and are therefore a complex, sacred person, who is fallen and lives in a fallen world and is subject to depression due to sin, ignorance, human frailty, wrong thinking, demon oppression, fear, and a lack of faith—but who has been given the remedy in knowing Jesus Christ, Lord of the universe through salvation? It really is a clear choice.

5

DEPRESSION AND SUICIDE

Any discussion about depression needs to consider the topic of suicide at some level. Those who commit suicide typically were diagnosed with depression prior to their death, so the two are inextricably linked. We saw earlier that even godly believers got so depressed at times that they no longer wanted to live in light of life's seemingly unbearable trials—believers like Job, Elijah and Jonah. Depression that leads to suicide is a major problem today in our country.

Suicide is a very controversial topic in the Christian community. Maybe you have been in one of those heated debates with fellow Christians at one time or another as one Bible-believer was adamant that suicide was the worst sin ever—the "unforgivable sin." They allege that anyone who commits suicide either loses their salvation or they showed by their selfish act that they were never saved in the first place. And then there are those who argue that suicide is a forgivable sin and in fact real Christians can commit that sin and still go to heaven.

It is true that suicide is one of the most self-centered acts one can commit, since Scripture says, "your are not your own...you have been bought with a price" (1 Cor 6:19-20). And God said emphatically, "Behold, all souls are Mine; the soul of the father as well as the soul of the son is Mine" (Ezek 18:4). No person has the right to end their own life. But at the same time, Samson, who is commended for being a man of faith (Heb 11:32), committed suicide. And godly men, David and Moses, were both guilty of murder—yet they were forgiven and "gained approval" from God (Heb 11:39; cf. 11:24, 32). So the suicide debate will continue.

But for our purposes here in discussing depression, let's look at a few statistical updates from the American Foundation for Suicide Prevention.[1] This group reports that there is one suicide every thirteen minutes, and over 100 per day in America. In 2016, there were over 40,000 suicides reported. It is the second leading cause of death between people ages 15-34. White males account for 70% of all suicides and the highest rate overall by age is among adults between 45 and 55.

---

[1] www.afsp.org/about-suicide/.

The world says depression that leads to suicide is a "mental illness," whatever that means. The Bible gives a more complete assessment of severe depression and suicide, which is based on a thorough biblical anthropology. Humans are persons made in God's image (Gen 9:6). Because of this, every human is highly complex, constituted to reflect God's communicable attributes—so every human is a rational, emotional, volitional, physical, social, moral, religious and spiritual being. This is in utter contrast to what the world says about the human makeup. People are not just a higher form of animal or the mere by-product of chance, having evolved from primordial slime millions of years ago.

Depression is not just some short-circuitry problem in the evolutionary process or only the result of chemicals being out of balance in our physiology. Depression is directly related to one's thought life (Prov 23:7), which directly impacts the emotions. Depression is also directly related to one's relationship with the Creator, for it is God who has brought every human being into existence, and made every human soul accountable to Him. The Holy Spirit declared this reality through the apostle Paul: "He Himself gives to all people life and breath and all things...in Him we live and move and exist" (Acts 17:25, 28).

A person trying to live this life in utter indifference to the Creator is like a fish trying to live out of water. There is an onset of fear, anxiety, hopelessness, panic, insecurity, and depression anytime humans try to live life independent of the God who made them. And the longer people push God aside, the bigger their problems become.

A person trying to live life without the God of the Bible, or without submitting to Christ the Lord, is a person who has no real hope, and hopelessness is at the heart of depression. Indeed, depression is the opposite of hope. Hope comes with knowing God. Proverbs says plainly, "The hope of the righteous is gladness" (10:28). The Bible is clear that the only real hope for the human soul is Christ, and the converse is true—those without Christ have no hope. Ephesians 2:12 says it this way: "remember that you were at that time separate from Christ, excluded from the commonwealth of Israel, and strangers to the covenants of promise, having no hope and without God in the world."

Judas is the prime example in the Bible and in human history of someone who experienced severe depression then committed suicide as a result of defying his Creator and rejecting Jesus the Savior. Judas betrayed Jesus to the Jewish leadership for thirty pieces of silver, after which he "went away and hanged himself" (Matt 27:5). His suicide was not a result of chemical imbalances in the brain, nor a result of a glitch in the evolutionary process, nor a result of bad parenting he received, nor a result of low self-esteem, nor a result of poor socialization. Judas' depression and suicide was the result of being a tormented soul. His suicide was the result of a long-term spiritual struggle deep within his soul wherein he chose to seek his own selfish desires, to go against his God-given conscience, and to reject unparalleled special revelation as he sought to find counterfeit fulfillment apart from Christ. In the immediate aftermath of his betrayal of Christ he was overwhelmed with his own guilt (Matt 27:3). Suicide is never the beginning of something— it's always the end result of a long journey away from God.

Depression and suicide became a national conversation when Academy Award winning actor Robin Williams committed suicide by hanging himself in his son's bedroom on August 11th, 2014. It turns out Williams had been struggling with severe depression for years and was on at least two antidepressants. Here was somebody who had everything that the world had to offer: success, fame, notoriety, wealth, influence, security—everything you could possibly want.

Ironically, he was the "world's greatest comedian" who made people laugh and feel happy, and passed himself off always as someone who could laugh at everything in life. On the surface, everything looked good, and he seemed content. His lifestyle and achievements were coveted by millions. Yet, deep within his soul, behind the veneer, there was emptiness. And then as the news came out the media began blaming it on depression, among other things, which was a surprise to many. Robin Williams didn't know Jesus Christ. He had been running from God for sixty-three years, and it finally took its toll.

Psalm 32:10 says, "Many are the sorrows of the wicked." That's a good definition of the chronic depression that Robin Williams suffered that resulted from years of deliberately living a life devoid of God and Christ. He couldn't run away from His Creator and the Judge of every soul (Ezek 18:4), and he ended up taking his own life. He was wicked at least up until he died—we don't know what happened in the last moment—but he lived his life in rebellion against God. You can watch YouTube videos where Williams makes a mockery of Christianity, blaspheming Jesus in his comedic routines to earn a laugh and a buck. The secular media completely ignored the spiritual demise of Williams and its implications on his depressed soul.

The Christian world has also had national discussions about depression and suicide. Not long ago, the whole world was talking about Matthew Warren, the son of Rick Warren, who at age 27, on April 5th, 2013, shot and killed himself in his home with a gun. Rick Warren is probably the most famous pastor in the world and is considered by many to be "America's pastor." A year after his son's death, Warren came out with an opinion article in *Time Magazine*, and here's what he said:

According to the National Alliance on Mental Illness, 60 million Americans experience a mental health condition every year. That's one in four adults and one in ten children. People of every race, age, religion or economic status are affected. Whether we are aware of it or not, we all know someone who is living with some form of mental illness. Mental illness is something we are intimately acquainted with, as our youngest son, Matthew, struggled with a variety of mental illnesses from a young age. Even as a toddler, there were signs that things were not right. At age seven, he was diagnosed as clinically depressed, which surprised us as we were unaware that children that young could be that depressed. As the years went by, he began to experience major depressive episodes as well as panic attacks, extreme mood swings, obsessions, compulsions, personality disorder, heartbreaking problems in school and relationships. Life became a painful revolving door of doctor appointments, medication therapy, and adjustments to school classes. There were periods of relative stability, but then Matthew's suicidal ideation became part of our daily life. Our hilariously funny, immensely creative, intensely compassionate son struggled to make sense of his life and the mental pain he was experiencing. His anguish was our anguish. On April 5th 2013, impulse met opportunity in a tragic way when our beautiful son ran into the unforgiving wall of mental illness for the last time.[2]

Since his son's tragic death, Rick Warren has written much and talked a lot about depression and suicide, seeking to offer his advice and to console those suffering from like experiences. One venue he uses for such purposes is his blog, Pastors.com. On August 14, 2014, one of the most popular blogs posted on that site had to do with depression and suicide in light of Robin Williams' suicide written by Allen White, a friend of Warren.

In this post, White is writing to pastors, exhorting them what to emphasize when it comes to talking about depression and suicide. In his three main points, he makes some startling and disturbing claims. For example, he assumes that depression is a "mental disease." Then he follows that unsubstantiated assertion by saying, "Mental illness is...incurable...it never goes away." And to top it off he writes in bold

[2] Rick Warren and Kay Warren, "Churches Must Do More to Address Mental Illness." *Time*, March 27, 2014.
http://time.com/40071/rick-warren-churches-must-do-more-to-address-mental-illness/, accessed May 16, 2018.

claiming, **"Finding Jesus is NOT the Cure for Depression!"**

When I first read this statement I was aghast. This is the exact opposite of what I believe. As a Christian and a pastor I am called to preach "the gospel"— "gospel" means "good news." The good news is that Jesus can save anyone from sin. And sin is the root to all the problems in this fallen world. Salvation in Christ gives real, internal, everlasting joy and hope. At salvation God imparts His Spirit into the believer, providing access to the fruits of the Spirit, which are "love, joy, peace, patience, kindness, goodness, faithfulness, gentleness, self-control" (Gal 5:22-23). These virtues all counter hopelessness, sadness and depression.

In God's providence, the same week I read this blog-post I had the privilege of baptizing a person at my church. Step one was for me to hear her testimony. For forty minutes, with great joy and some tears, she shared how Jesus had been working in her life over the course of years as she was exposed to the biblical gospel as believers witnessed to her and prayed for her salvation.

It all culminated in her radical transformation when she believed the gospel with understanding and she was born again (John 3:7). In His grace, God had made her a new creation (2 Cor 5:17). As an unbeliever she battled severe depression for years. In her testimony at one point she actually said, "Jesus saved me from depression!" I almost fell out of my chair upon hearing that, as I had just read the Pastors.com blog a couple days before, which dogmatically warned pastors that **"Finding Jesus is NOT the Cure for Depression."** It has been four years since she gave her testimony, and she continues to grow in the grace of Christ as a believer. She still believes that Jesus saved her from depression. She admits that life is still hard, since we live in a fallen world, but she recognizes that God in Christ is her sufficiency, even in the hard times.

The next chapter is actually her story. I include it as a testimony to the saving power of Christ and as an example of His complete sufficiency of what He offers in salvation. I trust you will be edified by what God has done in her life through His life-changing gospel and His powerful Spirit. When Jesus saves a sinner, He provides a complete salvation—redemption of mind, soul and spirit, and in the life to come, complete redemption of our bodies as well (Rom 8:23).

6

JESUS SAVES FROM DEPRESSION!

Growing Up Catholic

I was born and raised in a nominal Catholic home in California. I went through the typical "sacraments" including baptism as an infant, First Communion and Confirmation. I went to Mass and occasionally prayed on the rosary. As a teenager and young adult, I went to church mostly with my friend because my parents were attending less frequently. During all those years of attending Mass, I did not learn about the Bible; rather, the emphasis was on rituals and Catholic traditions. I don't remember much of what was taught specifically, but I do recall feeling guilty all the time.

As I look back, it is clear that I was plagued by bouts of depression from age thirteen until I was thirty—seventeen consecutive years of erratic emotional turmoil and hopelessness that covered me like a shadow that I could not shake. The episodes began as I entered my teens and seemed to progress worse and worse with time. The first traumatic episode of depression hit me when I was thirteen. Seemingly out of nowhere, I quickly got to a point where life did not seem like it was worth living—I had no purpose in life and I became very confused. In the confusion, being overcome with depression, and not having anywhere to turn for answers, at age thirteen I decided to end my life—I wanted an escape from this new onset of hopelessness that overwhelmed me. So in secret, I took a bottle of Tylenol and a can of beer to the bathroom and started consuming the pills until I passed out.

My younger sister found me passed out on the floor and my mom ended up rushing me to the emergency room at the local hospital. I spent most of the night at the hospital drinking a dark substance called activated charcoal that was supposed to help absorb the medication I swallowed. We tried to keep the incident a secret, but my school found out about it so I ended up talking to the school counselor on the phone the next day, trying to explain away and minimize what had just happened. I made up a story, which she believed. I didn't want to tell her or anyone about my depression and feelings of hopelessness, so I lied. I said I was feeling fine and would never do it again.

This was the beginning of a long, difficult journey

of depression and anxiety that would ultimately lead to a low and empty place in my life. I had bouts of depression for the rest of my teenage years. All through high school I resorted to alcohol in a futile attempt to drown the depression, and in my early twenties, my depression became severe again.

College Years

Upon graduation from high school, I entered college full-time and also started working at the bank full-time. Even though I was super busy with plenty to do and having not much idle time, I still had an ongoing battle with sporadic flare-ups of depression. During this period, suicidal thoughts became more real and regular. I would wake up feeling hopeless and unable to get out of bed. I would call in sick to work often because of my depression and would avoid being around people. These dangerous and ominous thoughts grew worse and worse, culminating in an event that transpired when I was twenty-two, just after I finished college.

One week in late December, feeling awful and just wanting the pain to end, I once again seriously considered ending my life. Ironically, at the same time, I was afraid of dying and had a fear of death. I was scared, so I called 9-1-1 and asked for help, telling them I was afraid I was about to hurt myself. The police responded imme-diately as they came and got me and took me to a psychiatric wing of the local hospital where I was placed on suicide watch. I was there for only a day because I was allowed to leave whenever I wanted since I checked myself in. I assured them I was "feeling" better, so they let me leave. It was Christmas Eve. The next day was Christmas and I went to celebrate with family, pretending all was normal. I didn't tell anyone anything and had become very good at hiding how I felt.

Around three years later, the depression and anxiety became even more severe, which was triggered by a life-threatening incident at work. While employed at the bank and working as a service manager, our location was held up by a gunman. He also was wielding a knife. In the mayhem, he violently grabbed me and took me hostage as he pressed the knife against my throat, demanding money from the tellers and bankers. He got what he wanted and left, with no one getting hurt. But, as a result, I was traumatized and could not overcome the brush with death at the hands of a murderer. The bank offered trauma care for any of the employees who needed psychological counsel or psychiatric care. It was apparent I needed both, so I took them up on their offer.

Panic

It was during this season of life that I started getting "panic" or "anxiety" attacks. I experienced shortness of breath and could feel my heart pounding, as though it were ready to burst through my chest. I thought I was going to pass out but eventually it would pass. My emotions and equilibrium were out of sync. I was having trouble sleeping. There was once a period of eight days when I did not sleep; I became delirious to the point of having hallucinations from sleep deprivation. In desperation I asked myself, "What if I just crash my car into a wall?" I was scared I would hurt myself or someone else if I listened to these thoughts, so I decided to let my therapist know. I was checked into the hospital on a suicide watch for 72 hours.

Over the next few years, I had a psychiatrist who gave me drugs, a psychologist and therapist who gave me psychotherapy, and I also participated in group counseling. It was at this time, thanks to the psychiatrist, that I began taking psychiatric drugs like the tranquilizer Klonopin, the sedative Ambien to help me sleep, and the antidepressant Prozac to help with my major depression. The medications had an immediate effect on my physiology, but as time went by, they did not help at all. As a result, my psychiatrist would just keep increasing the dosage. In addition, they recommended that I partake in "Intensive Outpatient Therapy" three weeks at a time, six hours every day. So I did—on three separate occasions over a three-year period. All this proved ineffectual as well in the end, as it did not "heal" me from my anxiety, depression, fear and hopelessness that had become the norm of my life.

Around a year later, I ended up in the hospital again. This time, it was for a whole week. They adjusted my medication type and dosage. I felt a little better for a while but, once again, anxiety and depression would come back to haunt me.

During those dark years, I would pray and beg God to take away my depression. I wasn't yet a Christian, but I did believe in God and begged for His help. I couldn't understand why God would allow this to happen to me and I thought He didn't care. Eventually, I stopped praying out of disappointment and frustration, and I also stopped going to Mass and began to just focus on myself and live for myself.

I focused on my career, material possessions, and just having fun—trying to get the most out of this life. But no matter how many things I bought, vacations I took, or promotions I received, it was never enough to sustain any real joy. It was all superficial and unfulfilling. I started reading self-help books to try to "find myself." I read books about pursuing happiness and watched videos on "The Law of Attraction" in search of the true meaning of life. It was all very self-centered. These books and strategies seemed to work for a few days or weeks, but none of them had lasting impact nor imparted real change.

A Breakthrough
One day while at home, when I was about twenty-eight years old, I called in sick because of my

depression. I watched an Oprah episode that featured a guest "spiritual guru" who talked about his life-changing book and video called *The Secret*. Oprah played clips of the video, which piqued my interest. As a result, I bought the book and video on the spot. In the video, the "enlightened" guru spoke about God in a way that caught my attention. A few days later, I found a set of books by the community trash bin at my condominium complex. The author of the books was the same man I had seen on TV just a few days ago that spoke about God.

The "coincidence" freaked me out a little, but I read the books anyway and it made me wonder if I should start going to church again. Today, I would not recommend *The Secret* to anyone, but God definitely used it to trigger my thoughts about spirituality and religion in a new way. I started visiting all kinds of churches and exploring various religions and denominations, including the New Age religion and even the teachings of the Dalai Lama, but nothing seemed right. I even went to an eclectic, ecumenical church that read from the Torah, the Qur'an, and the Bible. I tried going back to a Catholic church, but it seemed so empty to me. I began to cultivate a spiritual hunger and I felt a void that could not be filled.

It was around this time that I met the man who would become my husband. I was now thirty. He invited me to a non-Catholic church that talked about the Bible. I thought it was strange, but I kind of liked this new guy who asked me to go to church. I agreed to go to church with him but told him I was Catholic and that I didn't believe everything that was written in the Bible. He would try to convince me that everything in the Bible was true, and I would get irritated with him. But I kept going to church with him and just figured it was good for me. Over time, I thought the music was amazing, the pastor said some nice things, and I felt good after the church service.

The Power of the Word

Shortly after this, my Christian brother-in-law and his wife let me borrow a book entitled *Slave: The Hidden Truth about Your Identity in Christ*, by John MacArthur. When I started reading the book, it made me feel slightly uncomfortable, but at the same time I couldn't put it down. The book quoted Scripture, so I began to cross-reference it with the Bible. For the first time in my life, Almighty God allowed me to understand the true meaning of what Christ did for me when He was killed on the cross.

It became clear to me that the Bible taught that Jesus willingly died on the cross as a substitute for my sin, that He bore the punishment for sin that was meant for me, and rose on the third day. I saw that it was only through Him that we can have eternal life. I had heard and read this before many times, but its true meaning was never clear until that moment. God opened my eyes to see that we are either slaves to sin or slaves to Christ.

Up until this moment, I had been a slave to my own sin. I learned that being a slave to sin leads to death, but being a slave to Christ leads to eternal life. I understood this meant that my life was not my own. It was bought with a price, and now my life belonged to our Lord Jesus Christ. I felt a great weight lifted and an indescribable sense of peace. I remember begging God for forgiveness, thanking Him for what He did for me, and in my prayer I let Him know how honored I was to now be His slave and serve Him all the days of my life. It was through this experience that I became a born-again Christian and received total forgiveness of sin and eternal life. God had eternally adopted me into His family and made me a new person—not based on anything I did, but according to His mercy.

On and off my whole life I had been chasing a god that would fit my needs, but the true God of the Bible made me see that I was created to serve Him and Him alone. I am so grateful for this gift of salvation.

Made New

Second Corinthians 5:17 says, "Therefore, if anyone is in Christ, he is a new creation. The old has passed away; behold, the new has come." God has made me a completely new creation from the inside out. He has given me all new desires. He gave me the desire to find a Bible-based church where my husband and I can learn and grow. I now love going to church, reading God's Word, and enjoying fellowship with my brothers and sisters in Christ. I love to listen to teaching on God's Word every day. I look for opportunities to share the gospel. I desire to serve and help my husband and view my marriage as a way to honor God. This life-style is all new to me.

Shortly after my salvation, I reduced and eventually completely stopped my depression and anxiety medications. I still have short bouts of depression, but they are very different from those I had prior to my salvation. For one thing, I now have a deep seated inner joy that I never had before being saved—not a shallow passing sense of happiness that depends on my emotions or circumstances—but true, abiding, supernatural joy based on my personal relationship with the Creator who is my Savior. I still battle with my emotions. Even after being saved for about five years now, I still sometimes wake up feeling sad, with a lack of interest in doing anything and the desire to be left alone and not see anyone.

When I find myself feeling this way, I pray about it, I listen to teaching on what the Bible says about depression, and I try to focus on others instead of myself. I will text a few people and ask them how I can pray for them or I will remember prayer requests and start praying for them. I ask myself, "How can I serve others today?" and then I serve, mainly my daughter and my husband. I preach the gospel to myself and focus on God's promises. I read the Psalms I have written on a post-it note that I chose to study during times of sadness and/or anxiety. I listen to hymns that speak of God's attributes. I confess any sin to God, including my sadness and anxiety. I remember that Satan is real and that he is always on the prowl, trying to steal my joy through his lies—but he can't have my soul. I remember what God's Word says in Romans 8:28, "And we know that for those who love God all things work together for good, for those who are called according to his purpose." God orchestrates every event in my life, even suffering and trials. He is in control and uses it for my good and for His glory!

Most of the time, doing some or all of these things will take away my depression, but occasionally I have a lingering sadness. During those times, I just remember that this is not my home, that the aches and groanings of everyday life are mere longings for my true eternal home in heaven (Philip 3:20-21).

God has taught me much through my struggles with depression. My advice to anyone suffering from depression or anxiety is to remember that what you need most in life is hope, real heavenly hope. And the only place to find that hope is in the gospel of Jesus Christ. If you have not done so already, I invite you to believe in the good news of Christ. We are all born sinners, separated from God, who is the holy Creator. He is perfect and there is nothing we can do to be "good" enough to become right with God. Because

God is holy, He must judge and punish sin. But the good news is that God so loved the world that He provided a way for sinners to be reconciled to Him (John 3:16). He sent his only Son, Jesus Christ, who was fully God and fully man, to live a perfect, sinless life and die on the cross as a substitute for sinners like me. He rose on the third day and ascended into heaven and is now seated at the right hand of God and will return one day. God loves His people with an everlasting love, to the point that He willingly died for them (Rom 5:8). Surrender to God and give Him control of your life. In return, He will give you true, lasting peace and joy (Matt 11:28-30).

If you are a Christian and suffer from bouts of depression, I encourage you to turn to God's Word in the Bible and focus on His promises. Examine your prayer life, Bible reading time, any sin you may be harboring, and your thought life. We live in a fallen world and we are constantly bombarded by worldly and secular things, so we need to make sure we are feeding our spirit regularly: *"Man shall not live by bread alone, but by every word that comes from the mouth of God"* (Matt 4:4). Get your eyes off self and turn them on Christ. Fellowship with your brothers and sisters in Christ and find ways to serve others. "Do nothing from selfishness or empty conceit, but with humility of mind regard one another as more important than yourselves; do not merely look out for your own personal interests, but also for the interests of others"

(Phil 2:3-4). "Keep seeking the things above, where Christ is, seated at the right hand of God. Set your mind on the things above, not on the things that are on earth" (Col 3:2-3).

ADDITIONAL RESOURCES

For further study these resources might prove helpful:

Spiritual Depression by Matyn Lloyd-Jones

Anxious for Nothing by John MacArthur

Found: God's Peace by John MacArthur

Jesus and the Depressed by Steve Fernandez

Jesus Heals the Emotions by Steve Fernandez

Depression by Edward T. Welch

Christ and Your Problems by Jay Adams

The Biblical View of Self-Esteem by Jay Adams

What to do when you become depressed? (pamphlet) by Jay Adams

What to do when you worry all the time? (pamphlet) by Jay Adams

Loving God with All Your Mind by Elizabeth George

Lost Connections by Johann Hari (not a Christian book, but a helpful resource exposing popular false notions about depression)

ABOUT THE AUTHOR

Rev. Cliff McManis has been in pastoral ministry since 1989. He graduated from The Master's University with a B.A. in Biblical Studies and earned an MDiv from The Master's Seminary. He went on to earn his ThM and his PhD in Ecclesiology from the Bible Seminary in Independence, Missouri. He is the author of *Christian Living Beyond Belief*, *Apologetics by the Book*, and *The Biblically Driven Church* and editor and contributing author of *Rescued by Grace*. Dr. McManis is also a professor and board member of the Cornerstone Bible College and Seminary in Vallejo, CA. He has served in churches in southern California, Utah, Texas, and the San Francisco Bay Area, and has been an elder and the teaching pastor of Grace Bible Fellowship since its inception in 2006. He and his family currently reside in Northern California.

ABOUT GBF PRESS

GBF Press is the book publishing ministry of Grace Bible Fellowship of Silicon Valley. We started this publishing ministry out of the simple desire to serve our local body with substantive biblical resources for the sake of our people's growth and spiritual maturity.

But we also believe that book publishing, like any other Christian ministry, should first and foremost be under the supervision and accountability of the local church. While we are grateful for and will continue to support the many excellent traditional publishers available today–our shelves are full of the books they have produced–we also believe that the best place to develop solid, life-giving theology and biblical instruction is within the local church.

GBF Press is also unique because we offer our books at a very low cost. We strive for excellence in our writing and seek to provide a high-quality product to our readers. Our editorial team is comprised of men and women who are highly trained and excellent in their craft. But since we are able to avoid the high overhead costs that are typically incurred by traditional publishers, we are able to pass significant savings on to you. The result is a growing collection of books that are substantive, readable, and affordable.

In order to best serve various spiritual and theological needs of the body of Christ, we have developed three distinct lines of books. **Big Truth|little books**® provides readers with accessible, manageable works on theology, Christian living, and important church and social issues in a format that is easy to read and easy to finish. Our **Equip Series** is aimed at Christians who desire to delve a little deeper into doctrine and practical matters of the faith. Our **Foundations Series** is our academic line in which we seek to contribute to the contemporary theological discussion by combining pastoral perspective with rigorous scholarship. With our Foundations Series, we desire to bring theology back to the church and the church back to theology.

OTHER TITLES FROM GBF PRESS

Please visit us at GBFPress.com
to learn more about these titles

BIG TRUTH little books®
A Biblical View of Trials
Cliff McManis

What the Bible Says About Gray Areas
Cliff McManis

Faith: The Gift of God
Cliff McManis

How to Pray for Your Pastor
Derek Brown

The Problem of Evil
Cliff McManis

What the Bible Says About Government
Cliff McManis

God Defines and Defends Marriage
Cliff McManis

*Protecting the Flock: The Priority of
Church Membership*
Cliff McManis

*Educating Your Child: Public, Private, or
Homeschool? A Biblical Perspective*
Cliff McManis

Equip
*The Biblically Driven Church:
How Jesus Builds His Body*
Cliff McManis

*God's Glorious Story:
The Truth of What It's All About*
Colin Eakin

*Strong and Courageous: The Character and Calling
of Mature Manhood*
Derek Brown

The Gospel, the Church, and Homosexuality: How the Gospel is Still the Power of God for Redemption and Transformation,
Edited by Michael Sanelli and Derek Brown

Skillfully Surveying the Scriptures: Teaching the Bible Book by Book for Leaders and Laymen, Volume 1: Genesis-Esther
J. R. Cuevas

Foundations
Apologetics by the Book
Cliff McManis

81789780R00066

Made in the USA
Middletown, DE
27 July 2018